Moods of New Zealand Fly Fishing

JACKET AND BOOK DESIGN David Hallett
PRINTING AND BINDING Everbest Print Co Ltd
Published by David Hallett PO Box 26394 Epsom
Auckland New Zealand
Copyright 1997; David Hallett First published 1997.
ISBN 0-473-04622-9

Printed in Hong Kong

Moods of New Zealand Fly Fishing

Photographed and Published by
David Hallett

INTRODUCTION

It has been said so very, very many times over the years – perhaps first by Zane Grey back in the late 1920s – that it has nearly become a cliché. Flyfishing in New Zealand is arguably the best in the world. Or as Grey wrote, New Zealand is an angler's El Dorado.

Internationally recognised as among the finest trout fisheries anywhere, then, New Zealand has some reputation. But is it justified? Is it fair to say we have the best flyfishing on this, the third rock from the sun? Having fished in the United States, Canada and Australia but not as yet wet a fly in such other purported angling paradises as Russia, Argentina and Patagonia, it is difficult to say without some qualification that, yes, New Zealand's reputation is justified. Others with more experience than I, including those who have journeyed with rod and reel to all corners, even steadfastly maintain, without a hint of reservation, that New Zealand's trout fishing is not just among the finest, but it really is THE finest on the planet.

However lyrical people tend to wax about flyfishing here – and remember all anglers are born liars – it goes without saying that this place is special. Very special.

From around the world, avid anglers annually flock to our rivers, lakes and streams to cast to some of the most beautiful and well-conditioned rainbow and brown trout available. They come, of course, to lay claim to having fooled and conquered these wily fish and, on return to their homes whether here or overseas, these same anglers usually rejoice in their personal glory. They exasperate envious, and not so fortunate friends with their story telling. "I have fished New Zealand," they say. "I have fished mecca."

But catching fish in this freshwater antipodean aquarium is only part of the joy and charm of the New Zealand flyfishing experience. Arguably even more worthy of acclaim than our trout, or the size of our salmonids, is the environment in which these fish are found and pursued here.

New Zealand, and this can be said without hesitation or reservation, boasts incomparable pristine waters that lay or run in some of the most wondrous slices of outdoor heaven. Rivers and streams chortle through beech forests, spring creeks drain high country tussock lands as well as exquisitely green pastoral plots. Lakes shimmer in the shadow of mountain forests and reflect like mirrors in the face of sun-kissed glaciers. Huge braided beasts of rivers empty glacial valleys of their snow melt. Tiny tributaries, all fish filled, dot the landscape everywhere in both islands. No two rivers in this country are the same. No two give of their fish the same either.

Fishing New Zealand, then, is an experience like no other. You have the trout amongst the best anywhere. You have the environment – second to none. And you have the challenge – most of our trout are wild and notoriously difficult to catch.

But the experience is about much else as well.

Americans John Buchan and Paul Schullery share being among the most quotable of angling writers today. Both offer quotes that, while not aimed specifically to perpetuate New Zealand's assets as a flyfishing destination, do so admirably nonetheless.

Wrote Buchan: "The charm of fishing is that it is the pursuit of what is elusive but obtainable, a perpetual series of occasions for hope."

Wrote Schullery: "Fishing is a quest for knowledge and wonder as much as the pursuit of fish. A river or lake does not always give her fish, but the blessing of their company are always worth the trip."

Fishing in New Zealand is, as Buchan insists, "a perpetual series of occasions for hope." Not just hope that a huge clunker of a brown or rainbow might end up in the net, but hope that the back country experience, the time alone with nature, will not be elusive. In New Zealand, such awesome experiences cannot be elusive, except to the absolute pigheaded.

"The blessings" of the company of a river or lake, as Schullery insists, are nearly always worth the trip in Godzone, too. Even a cursory pause by anglers from casting, or mending, or wading in the wilds of this country to inspect the beauty around them brings dimensions to flyfishing that few other places can match. That is why this book by David Hallett is so important, so valuable. It is as the title suggests, about the moods of fishing New Zealand – not about the catching of fish, not about the how-to, nor where-to. It is about the experience. Even about the memory. The indelible memory that all angling adventures in this piscatorial paradise leave imprinted on our minds.

While I have not fished every pocket or piece of water photographed in this compilation, nor have I always caught fish in those places which I have been lucky enough to visit that are depicted within these pages, I am still able through the moods captured by Hallett, to feel a sense of belonging, or at least a sense of wanting to belong to the time and space of such magnificent angling locations. Solitude is at the very heart of all flyfishing for trout. We have that here in doses like no other place.

A friend once fished New Zealand with me – South Island and North Island. He came from the United States. He caught fish after fish – big ones, small ones, browns, rainbows. We fished lakes, tarns, streams, some waters so narrow and shallow they were more like ditches. We fished spring creeks, and steep glacial glides. On return he wrote to thank me for my time and hospitality, for taking him to paradise and back. He revisited a quote by Bill Barich on his return to Montana. It read: "I walked to the river and sat on the shore for a few minutes, just staring at the moonlight on the water. Moonlight never gets old."

My friend, in his letter of gratitude to me, then chose to paraphrase Barich's words, writing: "I have sat beside a New Zealand trout stream, just staring at the water. Flyfishing New Zealand never gets old." A book such as this not only perfectly perpetuates New Zealand's place at the top of world fishing destinations, it also ensures flyfishing New Zealand, even from your armchair, never gets old.

Bob South
Editor
Fish & Game New Zealand

Central Otago mountain stream

Wanaka wilderness

A dry fly Mataura evening

Late afternoon light on the Mataura

A Taupo wild rainbow

Tongariro River, Turangi

Morning fog rises off Lake Brunner

Day's end, Lake Brunner

Central North Island volcanic plateau

The Buller River, Nelson Lakes

Eglinton Valley, Fiordland

Motueka morning magic

Lake Coleridge, Canterbury

Dusk, Lake Taupo

A Nelson mountain stream

Rainbow's return

Mount Cook wonderland

Central Otago, Aspiring country

An evening on Lake Aniwhenua

Lake Rotoiti

An emerald pool on the Greenstone

Waioeka River

Twizel and the Ben Ohau Range

The snow-fed Stony River

Downtown Turangi

Alpine storm approaches

South Island's West Coast

Rain forest run-off

A lazy afternoon in Paradise

MacKenzie Country canals

High country hiking

Routeburn River, Glenorchy

Fiordland fantasy

In the shadow of the Earl Mountains

Evening on the lower Tongariro

Winter sunlight

The West Coast's Fox River

Summer on the upper Tongariro

Day at the office for Cedar Safaries

Kaweka high country

A good day on the Whirinaki

On a rock in a hard place 47

Fighting rainbow

Alpine playground

Ngaruroro stalking

Tussock lands of trophy trout

Horomanga hunter

Casting for rainbows in the Rainbow River

Rafting in the Rangitaiki

Ruapehu rainbow

Wilds of Waioeka

Casting to the cruising

Equine ride through glacial glide

Golden glow of autumn

Monumental Makarora

Mavora's magic moods

Among the willows of Coleridge

Cleddau River, Fiordland

Balmy days on Benmore

Lake Ida

The mist and rain of Milford

Storm clouds over the alps

At the Boyd, Kaweka Forest

A crystal clear Ngaruroro

Kaiiwi Lakes

Taupo traffic

Waipunga outback

A mossy grotto

Return to the wild

Winter on the Tongariro

Master caster

Tranquillity of Tarawera

A well conditioned rainbow

The waterfall pool

High country spring creek

Spring fed Deep Creek

Head waters of the Wanganui

Upper Tongariro River

West Coast spring creek

Rising to a mayfly

Four Mile River, Westport

In search of fighting rainbows

Early morning calm, Tarawera

Frosty dawn, Lake Tarawera

Reflections of Aniwhenua

The netted prize

Angling in the alps

Lake Hawea, Otago

94

Eglinton River, road to Milford

Spawning rainbows

The bountiful Buller

One Fly in the Wairau

Tutoko trout

Fishing among the ferns

Shimmery scene of forest green

Deep within the rain forest

Stalking Brunner browns

High in the Hokitika hills

The hunter and the hunted

Central North Island serenity

Busy in the Boyd

Pocket water on the Ohinemuri

Karangahake Gorge, Paeroa

North Mavora Lake, Southland

Fiordland's Cleddau River

Paradise,Glenorchy

A cautious approach

Beech forest of the Lewis River

Urewera mountain stream

The Wanganui above Kakahi

The upper Wanganui River

Summer on a silver stream

Tongariro solitude

120

Twilight on Lake Otamangakau

The grand scale of the MacKenzie Country

A fresh approach

New fly selected

A summer afternoon on the Buller

Fishing the Ngaruroro River

Central North Island high country

In the shadow of Mt Aspiring